The Stepmom Project

A 30-Day Personalized Journey for Stepmothers

ELIZABETH MOSAIDIS

Copyright © 2016 Elizabeth Mosaidis
All rights reserved.

No part of this book may be reproduced or transmitted in any form or by any means, electronic or mechanical, including photocopying, recording or by any information storage and retrieval system, without written permission from the author.

ISBN-13: 978-1540542120

Illustrations by Elizabeth Mosaidis

Author Photo by DM

Acknowledgments

Thank you to my family, friends, and colleagues for encouraging me to write this book. Thank you for the countless hours that you spent reading my book, editing it, and just listening to me talk about all of my book ideas.

A special thanks to my mom for editing my book over long Skype sessions.

Thank you to my husband for always supporting me in my endeavors and for bringing me breakfast in bed sometimes.

Thank you to all of you who shared your stories with me.

Dedicated with all my love to my parents, Gene and Suzanne Kohmetscher, for raising me in a loving household and encouraging me throughout my journey.

How to Use This Book: Read, Reflect, Experiment

You might be wondering if this book is for you. I wrote this book and compiled the information with the childless or childfree mother in mind. Since this creates unique challenges different from a blended family, I wanted to write a book focused on all of us out there who do not have children of our own.

You should also know this book is a little different. Why? This is not a book to be carefully handled. On the contrary, I encourage you to write and color in the book. Carry it around with you and fill the pages with your stories, reflections, and ideas. According to James Pennebaker, a psychology professor at the University of Texas at Austin, writing in a journal for 20 minutes a day has emotional and physical health benefits. Since writing has been proven to be therapeutic, you might want to use this book as a springboard for journaling, as a safe outlet to share your feelings and emotions. Paulo Coehlo said it best with this quote: "Tears are words that need to be written." I recommend setting aside about 20-30 minutes a day to read the advice, reflect on it, try out the action items, and write.

Alternatively, you might want to use this book as part of a weekly support group or with another friend, to get together and discuss the ideas. I would suggest reading through the material before your group meeting, jotting down some ideas, and then spending most of the meeting discussing the questions in detail. You can also hold each other accountable for the action items that you planned to try out each week.

Author's Note

To protect the privacy of certain individuals the names and identifying details have been changed.

Dear Reader,

I know how you might be feeling right now--how frustrated, hopeless, angry, or wistful. I know this because I have been there myself. You may be thinking things won't get better; that you won't have a positive relationship with your stepchild. But I also know you sought out this book and are looking for some encouragement, some help to get you through these tough times. Your journey through this book will help you feel better about the situation and gain control of your life and emotions.

Through my experiences and others, I'll share information that will help you get through these challenging days. Read each piece of advice, reflect on it, and make specific goals for the future as you go along. If you want to improve the situation, remain positive and work towards the daily goals that you set. Things will get better, but take it one step at a time and don't get too frustrated with the occasional setbacks that will happen. Instead of feeling depressed and helpless, take charge of what you can control in the situation. By taking action and making small changes, you will steer your life towards the goals that you have set.

I believe in you. You can get through this. I believe you have an incredible love for your husband that caused you to pledge your life to him, to be his until death. That you, at one time, believed that you could be happy with your husband and his children. You can. You just have to work a little harder and always keep this love in your heart and in your mind as you work your way through this book. I'm looking forward to embarking on this journey with you. You can do it! You're much stronger than you're aware of. You just need to find that strength deep within you and draw on it throughout this journey. It will get easier! Now, grab a cup of coffee or a glass of iced tea, take a few deep breaths, and let's get started.

Elizabeth

Connect with our Stepmother Community

You're not alone! Join us online at www.TheStepmomProject.com. Share stories of your new journey and gain access to resources to help you along the way. Of course, the best resources that we have are each other. Find a community to laugh, cry, and empathize with you.

Day 1: The Path to Becoming a Stepmother

Pursue some path, however narrow and crooked, in which you can walk with love and reverence.

-Henry David Thoreau

My path began on a dusty, rocky trail at Papago Park, a popular place for urban hiking. I had joined a hiking group, and nervous about joining the group for the first time, I had recruited my friend Christa into going on this first hike with me. We met up with a small group of hikers under a ramada near sunset. After brief introductions, we set off towards the rounded mountains as the sun was setting. "Check out that guy's calves," Christa whispered as we both happened to notice a tall, athletic man in front of us, talking to another guy. Secretly, I had been eyeing his legs as well, liking what I saw, so when he struck up a conversation with me later on about living in Greece and Germany, I was intrigued, especially since I had lived overseas before settling in Phoenix. We spoke briefly, enough for me to hope to talk to him again before he disappeared, apparently a faster hiker than me. After that day, I started to see him frequently on the hikes and made it a point to talk to him on the hike or at the Happy Hour spot afterwards. Something about hiking and seeing each other as our sweaty, natural selves made it easy for us to talk and get to know each other without the usual awkward dating conversations.

Soon, our relationship progressed, moving from chatting to officially dating. He mentioned having a five-year-old daughter, but I wasn't too concerned, being head over heels in love with him and just enjoying every moment that we spent together, painting couples' canvases, taking day trips to beautiful hiking spots and eating at romantic restaurants. I spent every other weekend alone because that is when Jim had his elusive daughter. He did not talk about her very much at first because he had negative experiences with dating women who did not want to talk about a child. Eventually, as I asked more questions, and he realized that I was genuinely interested in getting to know her, he opened up to the idea of me meeting her, so we set up a night to go out to dinner together at Sweet Tomatoes.

Before they arrived, I was extremely nervous, thinking about my potential stepdaughter (of course, I had already thought about marrying my boyfriend, and pictured our romantic life together.) However, I wasn't sure what to expect when meeting his daughter, since I knew that this meeting would affect our relationship. Being an optimist, I was prepared for the best, but that didn't stop me from having butterflies in my stomach and sweaty palms.

When they arrived, I wiped my sweaty palms on my jeans and opened my front door to see the handsome, athletic man that I had been dating, and a small, dark-haired little girl, partially blocked and peering at me from behind her dad's leg. This was the first time that I saw my boyfriend as a father and it was a heartwarming experience. As we rode to the restaurant, I turned around in the front seat to ask Emily about her teacher and her classes, and I could see her beginning to smile at me, losing some of her shyness as we chatted. We spent a lovely evening together, eating and laughing, and when my boyfriend dropped me off, I could tell that he was pleased with how the evening went. The next time we had a date, he presented me with three gorgeous blue orchids in a Japanese-style vase. Fast forward to a year and a half later, and we were walking down the same dusty trail at Papago Park at a sunset wedding, the sky so eye-catching that my husband said it was the most beautiful sunset he had ever seen.

Try It!
Take a moment and write down your path to becoming a stepmother. What is your story? How did you get here?

Reflection
♥ How did you meet your husband? What drew you to him?

_____

_____

_____

♥ When did you first meet your stepchild or stepchildren? What do you remember about that first meeting?

_____

_____

_____

My Story

Day 2: Fitting into Your New Roles

Be brave. Take risks. Nothing can substitute experience.
-Paulo Coehlo

After we got married, I sold my house, moved in with my husband and stepdaughter, beginning my new life as a wife and stepmother. I had been single for 33 years, spending part of that time traveling around the world teaching English, so the transition into my new roles was rocky for me. Even though I had spent time with my husband and stepdaughter, those times were more like "dates"—playing in the park, carving pumpkins for Halloween, flying a kite on a rare windy day. All of the things that adults secretly enjoy doing but might not do without a child around.

Now, I was picking Emily up from school, helping her with homework, making sure that she brushed her teeth, all of the mundane things that aren't so glamorous but a part of our daily lives. Suddenly, I felt the burden of being the best stepmother I could be. I felt guilty if I left Emily and Jim alone, so I stopped going to my Monday night Zumba class. Since I started helping Emily with her homework, I also stopped going to my yoga class.

Maybe it's partly because of all of the negative stereotypes about stepmothers or simply because of the pressure I put on myself, but I wanted to prove myself as a model stepmom to all of the other volleyball moms. Consequently, I went above and beyond. I made special Halloween goody bags for all of the girls on the volleyball team. I went to every practice and game because I didn't want the other mothers to think of me as the Wicked Stepmother. Rather than proving myself as Stepmother of the Year, I simply got burnt out trying to be the best that I could be. I was also starting to feel like a failure. I couldn't talk to my husband about this because I didn't want him to see me as a failure, so I decided to go to a counselor.

Try It!
Look over your "To Do" list and take some of the pressure off yourself by removing one of your items. Are you trying to do too much? Impress other mothers?

Reflection

♥ What changes did you go through when you got married? Did you move into a new house? Did you gain a new pet or pets?

_____
_____
_____
_____

♥ How did you react to these changes? How did your family members deal with the changes?

_____
_____
_____
_____

♥ Are you putting too much pressure on yourself? Are you getting burnt out?

_____
_____
_____
_____

Day 3: Something's gotta give.

Difficult roads often lead to beautiful destinations.

-Author Unknown

After being independent for so long and doing whatever I wanted, I was struggling with trying to take care of someone else and fitting into the new roles I thought that I had been assigned. Grappling with these new roles is a common challenge for stepmothers. As Jennifer, a stepmother to one girl, explained, "Balancing the needs of a new marriage with becoming an instant parent and instant family was the biggest challenge. Dealing with feelings of jealousy and trying to figure out how to handle conflict as an adult was also frustrating. I was so disappointed in myself for those feelings and didn't know how to cope."

If you're feeling this way, realize that you're not alone. Usually, couples have some time alone together before having children, but when you marry into a stepfamily, you don't have that time alone together. You need to learn how to deal with your new family members from the beginning. Jennifer went on to explain, "A wise counselor pointed out that there was no reason that I should automatically know how to manage these difficult feelings, and that I could learn new ways to cope and express myself."

My counselor helped me in a similar fashion by listening to all of my doubts and fears about becoming a new stepmother and then doing the best thing that she could have done for me. She gave me permission to be myself and keep doing some of the things that I had enjoyed before getting married. My counselor explained that I was mourning the loss of the person that I had been for 33 years, and even though getting married was a happy event, it was still a big transition in my life. However, I was losing myself by not doing the things that I enjoyed and made me "me." As a result, I felt weepy and emotional at home, not at all like my usual upbeat self. My counselor encouraged me to make a plan to improve things at home, so I could enjoy my new roles as stepmother and wife.

Reflection

♥ What do you remember about the first few weeks after becoming a stepmother? What was the transition like for you?
_____
_____
_____
_____
_____

♥ Did you have a breaking point? What was it?
_____
_____
_____
_____

♥ What helped you get through this period? Who did you talk to?
_____
_____
_____
_____

My Goals

_____
_____
_____
_____

Day 4: A Plan of Action

When it rains, look for rainbows. When it's dark, look for stars.
-Author Unknown

I made a plan to help me get through those tough times and learned a lot through this experience, what I am capable of and how strong I can be. I started by making an action plan with my counselor, with her holding me accountable in the next visit for completing those action items and asking me how it went. You can, too! Instead of feeling caught in the situation, angry and helpless, start making a list of action items to focus on each day or each week. These can be as simple as planning a weekend activity to keep you grounded and give you a little breather from your stepchildren. The first thing I did was talk to my husband and try to explain how I was feeling, how much pressure I had put on myself to be the perfect stepmother, and how, in trying to be perfect, I had lost myself. He was surprised to hear how I was feeling, but he was understanding and encouraged me to do all of the things that I had loved to do before marriage. So, for starters, I signed up for a weekly Zumba class and a yoga class. I began to feel happier, more like myself and felt like I was a good example for my stepdaughter, showing her the importance of doing things that you enjoy.

Try It!
Start by writing down two items that would make you feel better or help you to regain control over your life. Ask a trusted family member or friend to hold you accountable for these items by checking on your progress each week.

Reflection
♥ What would be an important aspect of your plan? What are some items that absolutely have to go into your plan?

_____

_____

_____

_____

_____

_____

♥ What would make you feel better? What would make you feel more like yourself?
_____
_____
_____

♥ Who can you confide in to hold you accountable for these action items on your plan?
_____
_____

My Plan

Day 5: Give it Time. Don't try to rush it.

All great achievements require time.

-Maya Angelou

Just as wine and cheese get better with age, so will your relationship with your stepchildren. "Let the kids be the one to open up to you. They will when they are ready," Sara, a stepmother of one year, advises. Try to have patience and let it evolve naturally. I know how hard this is to do because you hope to form a bond right away. However, research has shown that it takes about seven years for families to truly blend and become a family unit. Seven years might seem like a long time, but it will fly by and each year will get a little better. As Jennifer, a stepmother of 12 years, shared, "Now that my stepdaughter is older and in college, I really appreciate her for the amazing person she has become. I'm her biggest fan and enjoy the time we spend together." Just like Jennifer, you'll go through different seasons in stepmotherhood, with a unique set of rewards and challenges in each season.

The first year I made the mistake of planning a trip to Nebraska to introduce Jim and Emily to my extended family, but it was only a couple of months after we had gotten married. All three of us were still adjusting to our new family roles and it was overwhelming for Emily to meet so many new family members. Consequently, she acted up and made some hurtful comments about me, which I took very personally. Looking back on it now, I realize that it had been too soon after our marriage to plan such an important trip. We just needed more time together as a family before embarking on this trip. Had we waited a little bit longer, the outcome of the trip would have been completely different.

Try It!
Slow down. Think about an activity or event that you have planned that could be happening too soon. Can you postpone it until your family has had more bonding time together? When would be a better time to do it?

Reflection
♥ Have you had a similar experience with a vacation that turned out to be a disaster? Why was it a disaster? Were your stepchildren meeting new family members? Was this your first family trip?

_____
_____
_____
_____
_____
_____

♥ Have you had an experience with something that you tried to do as a family that was just "too soon?" What happened? How could you do things differently next time?

_____
_____
_____
_____
_____
_____

Day 6: Define your role with your husband and your stepchildren.

We delight in the beauty of the butterfly, but rarely admit the changes it has gone through to achieve that beauty.

-Maya Angelou

Part of the difficulty with your new role is that it can be hard to define and figure out exactly who you are and what you should be doing. Should you be getting involved with decisions about the child, such as whether to sign the child up for sports? Should you go to parent-teacher conferences? These questions and more will come up unexpectedly and you'll have to make some quick decisions. The first year is the hardest in figuring out your role and where you fit in because your husband and stepchildren have been operating for awhile without you, so they might not think of you when some of these questions come up. I remember the first year we were married, my husband called me at work to ask if I wanted to attend parent-teacher conferences with him. He hadn't thought of asking me until the last minute, and he didn't want to hurt my feelings but wanted me to feel welcome. I decided not to go because I thought it might get complicated with two sets of parents there when the focus should be on Emily and what's best for her. I thought that my husband could communicate all of the necessary information to me, and he supported me in my decision. The important thing is to keep open lines of communication when these situations come up and think about what is best for the child.

In the beginning, your role might feel rather nebulous, but after you give it some time and settle into your life with your new family, you'll figure it out, and so will they! Over time, my husband has started asking me more frequently for my opinion or input on situations involving Emily. In turn, I've felt more comfortable in my role, as well as a sense of belonging in my new family unit.

Try It!
Write down a description of your role within the family unit. How do you see yourself? What do you see yourself doing? How do you belong?

My Role

_____
_____
_____

_____
_____

Reflection

♥ Look over the description that you wrote down. Are you happy with it? How would you change it?
_____
_____
_____

♥ What kinds of questions regarding your role have come up so far? How did you handle these situations? How would you handle them differently in the future?
_____
_____
_____
_____
_____

♥ How has your role changed since you first got married?
_____
_____
_____
_____
_____

Day 7: Establish clear rules and routines.

It is not fair to ask of others what you are not willing to do yourself.
                                                                    -Eleanor Roosevelt

This is a big one because this can create or upset the harmony in your home. In general, everyone in your household will feel a greater sense of balance and stability by having clear rules and set routines. Talk to your husband about your expectations for your stepchild and come to an agreement on rules and chores. Make sure that everyone understands the rules, and depending on the age of the child, write them down for the child. Refer back to the rules to ensure that the child is clear on what is acceptable at your house. Remember that your child might have different or more relaxed rules at the other house, which is out of your control, but you can enforce rules that have been established at your house. You and your husband should always present a united front to the child, with any disagreements on discipline happening when you are alone as a couple.

Most research suggests that the biological parent should be the primary disciplinarian, with the stepparent supporting the biological parent in enforcing the household rules. Since discipline requires trust on the part of the child, trust that their parent loves them and is doing the best thing for them, most experts recommend giving time to let the relationship between the stepparent and child grow stronger and to build trust before the stepparent starts disciplining the child. If a stepparent is stricter than the biological parent and starts disciplining the child before trust develops between the stepparent and child, the child can feel resentful and this can damage a new, and often fragile relationship. This is why it is crucial for you and your husband to agree on rules and expectations and work together as a team to enforce them.

Try It!
Have a discussion with your husband about rules that your families had as you were growing up. Ask your husband specific questions about how he was raised: how he was disciplined, who was the disciplinarian—his mother or father, and how he felt about his upbringing. Asking these important questions about a person's past can help you understand how their past affects their current parenting style and/or decisions. Then set rules and routines for your stepchild with your husband and communicate them to the child.

Reflection

♥ What kinds of rules did your family have as you were growing up? Which ones do you think were important?

_____
_____
_____
_____
_____

♥ As a child or teenager, did you ever get in big trouble? How were you punished? How did you feel about that?

_____
_____
_____
_____
_____

♥ How has your stepchild reacted to the rules and expectations that your household has set?

_____
_____
_____
_____

♥ How do you and your husband work together to make sure that your stepchildren follow these rules?

_____
_____
_____
_____
_____

Day 8: Don't feel like you have to assume all responsibilities as the stepmom.

It takes a village to raise a child.

-African proverb

Your husband managed as a single parent for the months or years before you got married, so he can handle and is probably used to taking care of the children. You are not. Especially as a woman without children of your own, this is a new frontier for you. Your husband has already established routines with his children and is comfortable caring for them. Let him continue to do this and slowly start helping out and pitching in as you can. He will appreciate anything you can do to help, and you will be able to ease into your new role without getting burnt out. Some examples of things you can do to ease into your role are picking your stepchild up after school once a week, making a brown bag lunch for school, or reading before bedtime one night. I like to prepare Emily's lunch the night before because mornings are so rushed, and sometimes I'll put a chocolate or a note in there to brighten her day. My husband appreciates this because it makes the morning go a little more smoothly, and it's one less thing that he has to worry about.

Try It!
Start slowly by taking on a new responsibility or helping out with a task this week.

Reflection
♥ Which new responsibility did you take on this week? How did it go?
_____
_____

♥ How did your husband and stepchild respond to this?
_____
_____

♥ What would you like to try next week?
_____

Day 9: Plan ahead.

Sometimes you will never know the value of a moment, until it becomes a memory.
-Dr. Seuss

An entire weekend with your stepchild might feel a little daunting at first. Should you spend the time as a family unit? Should you give your stepchild time alone with your husband? The answer, according to researchers, is yes and yes. The general rule of thumb is that the parent and stepparent should each try to spend at least 10 minutes of quality time alone with the child a day. This can be challenging, especially on busy weekends with sports activities and other commitments, but aim for those 10 minutes as frequently as possible to bond with your stepchild.

You should also plan at least one activity each weekend for the whole family, something that you can all enjoy doing together. This can be as simple as playing a game of Monopoly, having a family movie night, or concocting a special smoothie recipe together. The important thing is that you spend time together and learn how to interact as a family unit.

My husband and I usually make a plan with 1-2 activities for the weekend before we have Emily. We'll decide on a family activity and some loose ideas of what to do for individual activities, although most of the time, the individual activities for Emily and I usually involve some type of crafts. Jim and Emily like to go to the Saturday morning workshops at Home Depot or challenge each other to a game of Chinese Checkers. As for family activities, we like to check out local festivals or spend some time on the hiking trails. One of our favorite family activities involved a trip to a nearby ostrich ranch. We still laugh about how we fed the ostriches from a platform by dangling oranges slices in front of them with a fishing pole. This is a family memory that we'll reminisce about for years to come.

Try It!
Make 1-2 plans for the upcoming weekend. What would you all enjoy doing together? You can even start a family notebook with ideas of what your family can do together in the future. Write down your ideas and make them happen!

Reflection
♥ What kinds of activities do you like to do with your stepchildren?
_____
_____

♥ What kinds of activities does your husband enjoy doing with his children?
_____
_____

♥ Think about a particularly fun family outing with your new family. What made it so enjoyable?
_____
_____
_____
_____

♥ What would you like to try doing together in the future?
_____
_____

Day 10: Give yourself permission to make mistakes.

Life is like riding a bicycle. To keep your balance, you must keep moving.
-Albert Einstein

One thing that I've discovered the hard way is that "no" is a difficult word to say when you want your stepchild to like you. When Emily would ask me if she could have an extra cupcake or if she could stay up a little bit later, I had a difficult time saying "no." Of course, my common sense would tell me that kids need to hear "no," but at the same time, that yearning for her to like me would overtake my common sense, and I would say yes. Soon, Emily started to see me as a pushover, so she would ask me instead of her dad. This is a typical mistake that stepmothers make in their quest to garner their stepchild's affection. Sara, a stepmother of three children, echoed this sentiment. "I wanted the kids to like me, so saying no was hard. I didn't want to disappoint them," she explained. However, Sara also learned that it's important to set boundaries with the children. She went on to say, "It's okay to say no sometimes. You want the kids to have respect for you and not walk all over you."

This is just one example of mistakes that stepmothers make as they're figuring out their new roles. Remember that there is a learning curve with any new role, so it's natural to make mistakes. Don't beat yourself up if you don't get it right the first time. You might be tempted to give up when you make a mistake and things get rough, but keep trying and learn from your mistakes.

Try It!
Think about one mistake that you have made in the past and make a conscious note to do things differently next time.

Reflection
♥ Do you have a hard time saying "no" to your stepchildren? If so, when?
___
___
___

♥ Looking back, what kinds of mistakes have you made? What did you learn from them?
___
___
___
___
___

♥ How can you approach these situations differently next time?
___
___
___

Day 11: Find something in common.

When you do things from your soul, you feel a river moving in you, a joy.

-Rumi

"My stepdaughter and I bonded over our love for my husband and her father," Laura, a stepmom of four years, divulged over lunch. "We both enjoy teasing him about his idiosyncrasies," she explained with a chuckle. Your love for your husband and your stepchild's love for his or her father is a great foundation, but also try to find something else that you and your stepchild have in common. This could be a hobby, a passion for collecting postcards, or an ice cream store that you both love. No matter how difficult your stepchild is, you must be able to connect on some level. Maybe you both enjoy eating cupcakes from that special bakery down the street, or maybe you both love to watch *Shark Tank* in the evenings. Liz, a stepmother of 11 years, advises stepmothers to "make special time for your step children and make sure the time is individual to each child." Liz explains, "Anthony and I are both sushi lovers so our special time is sushi almost every other week. We take turns paying because now he is 27 and lives on his own in his own house." This is a special bonding time for Liz and Anthony when they can share tidbits about their daily lives, while also sharing their love for sushi.

If it's something that you both enjoy doing, you'll have a good time, regardless of whether you always get along. Emily and I both love to do crafts, so on the weekends, we'll normally work on a craft project. Since we're both focused on our projects, we might chat while we're working, or a comfortable silence may settle between us as we're concentrating on our projects. The best part is that we have a finished product at the end of our time together, a memento of our time spent toiling over our crafts. Later on, we'll reminisce about the crayons that we melted together, or the button bowl, when we painstakingly glued buttons to a balloon and then re-glued them when they fell off. As we look around the house, we can see these artifacts from our time together, making our home cozy and uniquely "ours." We also enjoy giving them to people we love and sharing how we made them.

Try It!
Take a moment and brainstorm some of the things that you and your stepchild have in common. Don't hesitate—just write down whatever comes to mind; the more ideas, the better!

Now, take a look at your list and start small. Choose one thing and make a plan with your stepchild to do that activity or go to that restaurant together. Remember that this should be something that you enjoy as well, so have fun with it!

Try It!

_____
_____
_____
_____
_____

Reflection
♥ What is something that you and your stepchild enjoyed together in the past? What made it so enjoyable?
_____
_____
_____
_____

♥ What do you enjoy doing when you have some free time? What does your stepchild like to do?
_____
_____

Day 12: Laugh when things don't go according to plan.

One loses many laughs by not laughing at oneself.

-Mary Engelbreit

Picture yourself taking your stepdaughter to an art class that took three months to get into and the only reason that you were able to go is because someone canceled and you were next on the waiting list. You had it all planned out in your mind: she, your stepdaughter, would *love* the class, being the artsy child that she is and the two of you would bond over the shared experience of painting and interacting with the other families. Reality: your stepdaughter gets bored within the first 5 minutes and the activity that you had planned months ago and built up in your mind is a total loss. You go home disappointed and your stepdaughter goes home bewildered as to why you are so quiet. This is an example of one of my first experiences with feeling disappointed about something that I thought would be fun for both of us, a bonding experience. What I didn't realize at the time was that these things aren't personal. Emily's disinterest with the class wasn't a reflection on me as a stepmother. Sometimes things just don't turn out to be as fantastic as we plan them and build them up in our minds. Does that mean that we stop planning them? Absolutely not.

Recently, I had the brilliant idea of having breakfast for dinner. Emily had survived a big testing week at school and my husband had been busy at work. So I thought it would be fun for us to do something a little different and have pancakes, eggs, and sausages for dinner. My husband is the usual cook in our family, as I barely get near the stove. We have a running joke about how I might push the wrong buttons on the stove because one time I had accidentally turned it off while I was cooking. Anyway, I was determined to make pancakes, even though this would be my first experience making them. Couldn't be that hard, right? My mom and grandma had made them all the time growing up. So I poured vegetable oil into a large skillet and starting making them. Unfortunately, the pan started smoking right away due to the high heat and the oil, so our house quickly filled with smoke. My husband brought two fans into the kitchen from the garage and we opened all of the doors and windows to try and air it out. Do you know how long it takes to get that burnt pancake smell out of the house? About 4 days, to be exact. Meanwhile, my eyes are burning and I can barely see the pan. I enlist the support of my husband to make the eggs and sausage, but neither one are his forte, so he proceeds to cook the eggs without putting any oil or butter down, so they come out burnt and stuck to the pan, while the sausages also turn black around the edges. We all sit down to eat dinner through the smoke, with our cat sitting outside, looking in at us crazy humans, wondering how we could survive in all of that smoke. We ate very little, mostly because everything was burnt, but we all got excited later that night when we made smoothies for dessert. And those tasted delicious! The best thing about this night was that it was a bonding experience. We all laughed, and now we have an inside joke: how about breakfast for dinner?

Isn't that part of what makes families feel like families: shared experiences, laughs, and inside jokes? So the next time an activity or a day doesn't go as planned, remember that these days can only go as well as your attitude goes towards what happens. If you are disappointed and upset, that will be the mood that permeates the day. However, if you decide to laugh about it and move on, you'll be much happier, as will your family.

Try It!
The next time something doesn't go as expected, laugh it off. Make a joke and move on.

Reflection
♥ Think back to an activity that you were excited about that turned out differently than you expected. Why did it turn out differently?

_____

_____

_____

_____

♥ How did you handle the situation? Is there another way that you could have handled the situation to have a different outcome?

_____

_____

_____

_____

Day 13: Your new family is unique.

Every snowflake is unique, yet they are each perfect.

-Donald L. Hicks

Don't feel like you need to have the same type of relationship bonds that your family had growing up. In fact, by having expectations that your new family will be the same as your family growing up, you're setting yourself up for disappointment. This also applies to the relationship between you and your stepdaughter. Don't expect it to be the same as the relationship that you have with your mom.

I made this mistake when I first became a stepmom because I tried to be the kind of mom that my mom has always been to me. My mom was a stay-at-home mom and radiated loving kindness, even while raising three children very close in age. My mom and I have always had a close connection, and I thought I should have the same connection with Emily. So I tried really hard. But it felt forced and unnatural, and I realized that I should let it develop naturally. Just think of your relationship with your stepdaughter as a fragile flower that you are nurturing with love, patience, and kindness over time.

Similarly, oftentimes stepmothers have false expectations that their stepfamily is going to be the same as a biological family, which is not realistic. Stepfamilies and biological families have different dynamics within the family, and stepfamilies have unique issues that biological families don't have, such as parenting schedules, separate holiday plans, and custody issues. Instead of trying to emulate a biological family, find the beauty in your stepfamily and make the most of it.

Try It!
Write down three things for which you are grateful regarding your new family. Try to include something for each member of your stepfamily.

26

 1.

 2.

3.

Reflection

♥ Did you have any expectations about your stepfamily being the same as a biological family? If so, what were they?
_____
_____
_____

♥ What was your mother like as you were growing up? How would you describe your relationship with her?
_____
_____
_____
_____
_____

♥ Does your relationship with your mother affect your relationship with your stepchild? If so, in what way?
_____
_____
_____

Day 14: Make the most of your time without your stepchild.

It is fun to have fun but you have to know how.

-Dr. Seuss

While making the most of the time that you have with your stepchild is important, making the most of the time you have alone with your husband is also crucial. With the added stress of the dynamics within your new family, a strong bond between you and your husband will be particularly important to keep your family together. You'll want to plan a fun date night—a dinner, movie, jog, or a night out salsa dancing—on a regular basis when you don't have the kids to maintain that intimacy and closeness that you had when you got married. In the midst of arguments and unpleasantness that can arise from your parenting roles, the joy that you had spending time together when you were dating can become tainted when you get married, as well as being centered around the child. Don't let that happen. Guard your relationship with your husband and care for it just as you would with any precious resource. Maintaining the love that you have for each other requires time and effort, especially when you might be tired after a weekend with stepchildren. Shake off the exhaustion and any unpleasantness and make the most of the time that you have with your husband. Fall in love all over again.

Try It!
Plan a special night or even a romantic weekend getaway on a weekend when it's just the two of you.

Reflection
♥ What did you and your husband like to do when you were dating?

___
___
___
___
___
___
___

♥ What do you and your husband like to do now when it's just the two of you?
___
___
___
___
___

♥ What would be a romantic weekend getaway for the two of you? Where would you go?
___
___
___
___

Day 15: Create your own family traditions with your new family.

Happiness must be grown in one's own garden.

-Mary Englebreit

When Emily and I were preparing to decorate the tree last year for Christmas, I brought out all of the special ornaments that my parents had saved for me throughout the years; finally giving them to me when I got married. As we were hanging them, I shared some of the stories behind the ornaments and why they were special to me. Emily enjoyed handling all of the unique ornaments and hearing the stories because she was accustomed to only hanging generic red and silver ball-shaped ornaments, while I enjoyed sharing the stories with her because I felt like she could understand me better, how I was raised, little pieces of me.

When we finished decorating the tree, she looked over the tree and declared that something was missing. As we looked through my husband's decorations, we found bags of candy canes. "That's it!" Emily exclaimed. "We can't finish decorating the tree until we hang the candy canes," she said excitedly. So we hung the candy canes up, a new tradition for me, with all of the ornaments, and as we looked at the tree, I knew this would become our new family tradition.

Think about your family while you were growing up and what you normally did for birthdays, holidays, and special occasions. Now think about your new family. What traditions can you establish in your new family that will uniquely belong to your new family unit? These new traditions can be a melding of previous family traditions to suit your new family. This family tradition can be for a holiday, but it can also be a simple weekend tradition. Waffles on Saturday mornings with hot cocoa? Sure! Family Movie Night on Friday nights? Why not?

Try It!
Share some of your favorite family traditions. Ask your stepchildren and husband about their family traditions. Then create a new family tradition with your family.

Reflection
♥ What traditions did you enjoy as a child?
_____
_____
_____
_____
_____
_____

♥ What traditions have you started with your new family? What would you like to try in the future?
_____
_____
_____
_____
_____
_____
_____

Day 16 Appreciate the small things.

Train yourself to find the blessing in everything.

-*Author Unknown*

"You're the best stepmother ever!" Emily exclaimed after I threw a surprise luau party for her 9th birthday. Amazing how much one small comment can warm your heart and make all of the hours of planning the games, getting the food, making goody bags, and getting ready for guests, all worth it. I savored this moment and filed it away, ready to conjure it up during tough times down the road.

Another special moment was during Mother's Day this year. Normally, my husband takes Emily to the store to pick out a bouquet of flowers or balloons for me, but this year was different. Emily thought of me on her own and she made something special for me that she knew I would like. She looked through one of her craft books and found a tutorial for making a type of "Tea Cozy," consisting of fabric filled with cinnamon and nutmeg. When you put a cup of tea on it, the aroma from the sweet spices fills the room. This is special because Emily and I have a nightly routine of having a hot cup of tea in the evenings, so she knew that I would like it. She also made the sweetest card for me that I have hung up in my office, so I can look at it and be reminded of how much she loves me.

Appreciating the small things works both ways. When I recently made a trip to Barnes and Noble to pick out a birthday gift for my niece, I spotted some scratch and sniff doughnut stickers. Emily *loves* doughnuts! I wasn't sure if she would like stickers because she seems to have outgrown that phase, but when I brought them home, she snatched them up immediately and carried them around all weekend. I was surprised that she liked them so much, but was also pleased that she appreciated such a small gesture.

Try It!
Start a "Blessings" jar and have all members contribute to the jar throughout the year. On New Year's Day, open the jar and have each family member draw out a blessing and read it. Repeat until the jar is empty. This is the ideal time to reflect on all of your family's blessings from the past year. You can even make a scrapbook page showcasing all of the blessings from each year.

Reflection

♥ When was the last time you did something that your stepchild really appreciated? What happened? How did that make you feel?

_____
_____
_____
_____
_____

♥ When was the last time that your stepchild did something that you really appreciated? What happened? How did you express your appreciation?

_____
_____
_____
_____
_____

My Goals

_____
_____
_____
_____
_____
_____

Day 17 Put yourself in their shoes.

Don't worry about walking a mile in my shoes, just try a day thinking in my head.
-Author Unknown

This is a tough one for all of us because you can't fully understand what someone is going through until you've actually been through it yourself. I have tried to think about what Emily might be feeling about having a new stepmother, but since my parents aren't divorced, I can't truly relate to how she might be feeling. To try to gain a glimmer of understanding, I talked to some of my friends of divorced parents and found blogs and books online to see things from their perspective.

After interviewing children of divorced parents, I found that holidays are a difficult time for those children because they feel torn about which parent to be with during the holidays. Even though a parenting schedule is in place with holidays accounted for, the children can feel guilty when they are with one parent and worry about the other parent. They might fret about if the other parent has someone to spend the holiday with or if that parent is lonely.

Children of divorced parents also worry about how to balance relationships with their biological parents and stepparents. Lesley, an adult child of divorced parents, explained, "The thing I struggle with is not hurting my mom's feelings by expressing my feelings for my stepmom. I have a pretty good relationship with my stepmom. I didn't grow up in the house with her, so we don't have a lot of problems between us." When asked about what advice she would give to a new stepmother, Lesley went on to say, "Love your step children as you would your own and understand that they love you, too. They might not appreciate it now, but they will later."

Try It!
Try to think about the situation from your stepchild's perspective. If you're having a difficult time doing this, read a couple of blogs or articles written by adult children of divorced parents. Or, better yet, talk to a friend or family member whose parents divorced when they were young. Interview them—find out about the joys and the challenges.

Try It!

Reflection

♥ What did you find out after reading the blogs and articles or talking to others whose parents divorced when they were children?

♥ Did this change your perspective? Will you approach anything differently after considering another point of view?

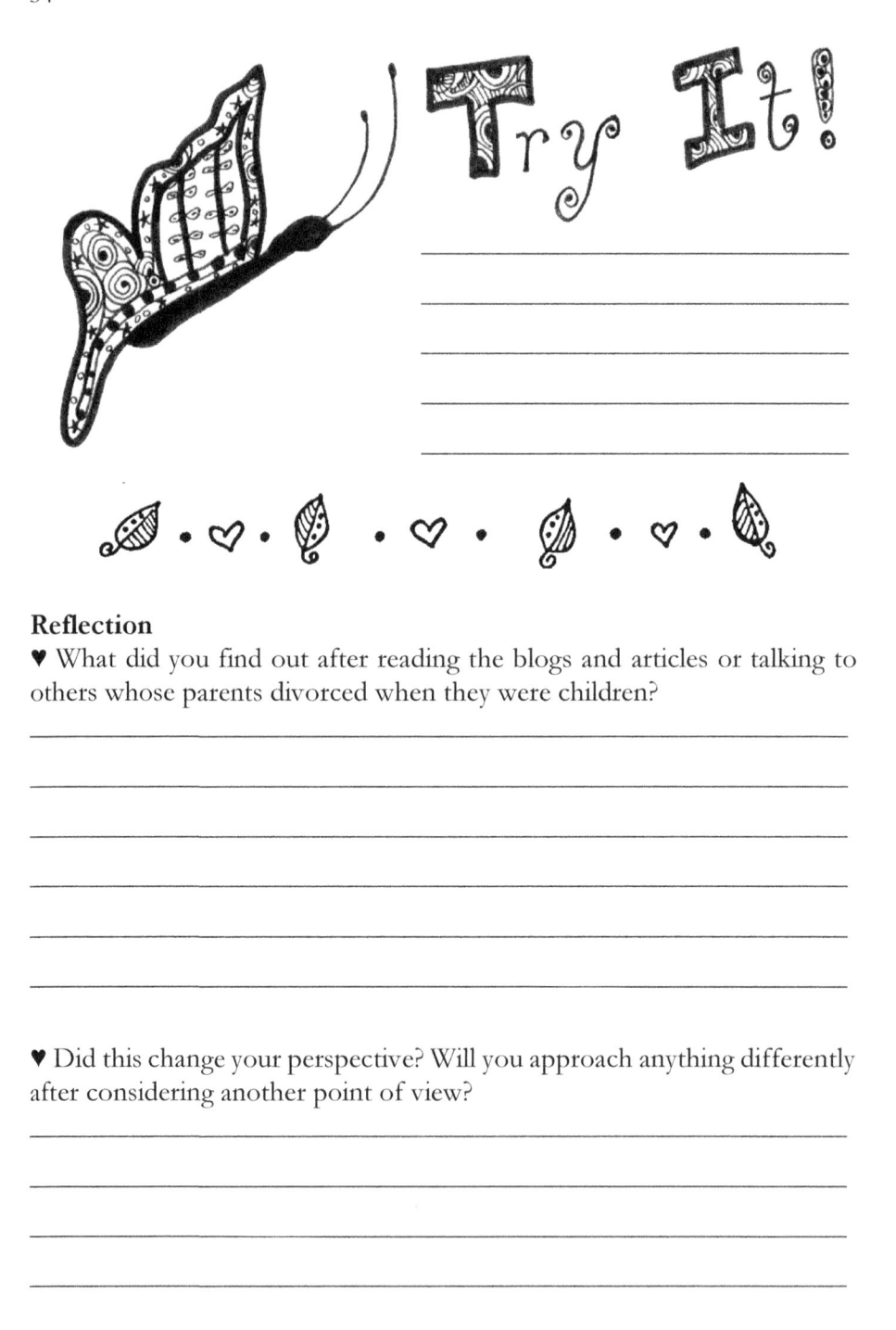

Day 18: Treat your husband's ex-wife in a business-like manner.

Step with care and great tact, and remember that life's a great balancing act.
-Dr. Seuss

Until this point, we have focused primarily on your relationships with your stepchild and your husband because you need to have a strong foundation to build on. This strong foundation will help you deal with the other aspects of your new life that may leave a bad taste in your mouth. The important thing is not to end up bitter yourself, so try to approach your husband's ex in a business-like fashion, much as you would interact with a difficult colleague at work.

The challenge for me has been not letting my husband's ex-wife sour or influence my relationship with Emily. Sometimes, my husband and I will spend wonderful, quiet weekends together, and then we'll get Emily and her mom will complain about something that happened, or about not sending the proper clothing, among other things. So, sometimes it seems as if drama and unpleasantness go hand in hand with Emily and her mom. However, I have made a conscious effort to separate the two and to think about how difficult it must be for Emily's mom to have another mom-like figure in the picture. I have been clear with Emily that I am not trying to replace her mom, and I do not try to infringe on mother-daughter things that Emily's mom might like to do with her. I simply try to be a positive influence in Emily's life.

Overall, I have found that keeping interactions with my husband's ex-wife at a minimum has been the best approach to this difficult relationship, for both my husband and me. My husband mainly communicates through emails, since calling and texting became excessive and sometimes involved name-calling or harassment. We also keep face-to-face contact to a minimum, since these interactions could also quickly deteriorate with off-handed comments made in the heat of the moment. My husband communicates the necessary information about Emily without being overly friendly or trying to plan joint activities together. We've simply found that the less interaction we have, the better it is for all parties involved.

With this in mind, one important point to remember is that you should never badmouth or say anything negative about your stepchild's mother.

Your stepchild's natural instinct will be to defend his or her mother, even if what you are saying is true, so you should never say anything negative about the child's mother. Let the child make their own determination about their parent. Research has also shown that saying negative things about a child's parent will make them feel anxious and affect their self-esteem because the child will wonder if they share the same traits as the parent that you are badmouthing.

Try It!
Try to separate the unpleasantness that may come from your husband's ex-wife from your stepchild. As hard as it may be, do not let those negative interactions influence how you feel about your stepchild. Keep interactions with your husband's ex-wife to a minimum.

Reflection
♥ What kind of relationship do you have with your husband's ex-wife?
___
___
___
___

♥ What difficulties have you had with your husband's ex-wife? What can you do to combat these difficulties? Would limiting interactions with her help this situation?
___
___
___
___

♥ How do you approach interactions with a difficult colleague at work? How can you apply the same principles to your interactions with your husband's ex-wife?
___
___
___

Day 19: Apply your career skills to your role as a stepmother.

What could we accomplish if we knew we could not fail?

-Eleanor Roosevelt

Kill them with Kindness. I encountered this quote on the bottom of a Snapple iced tea one day as I was having an exceptionally rough day with one of my students. As a teacher, I am committed to reaching all of my students, regardless of their behavior, but I had one student that acted up, no matter what I did. I talked to him after class, I asked him how I could support him (this was at the college level), but he persisted in his bad behavior.

He disrupted the class, and the other students did not want to work with him. Even though he tested me time after time, I never let him know that he was getting to me. I reminded myself to be consistently firm but fair. On the last day, he wrote a letter to me in his journal and apologized for his behavior. He wrote, "Sorry for all of the hard times you've been through because of me. It was a good test for your patience. You did well."

I keep this experience in mind as particularly trying days come up with Emily. Since teaching comes naturally to me, I try to apply those teaching skills to my interactions with Emily. Even though she is not my student, I approach certain situations as teachable moments and try to think about how I can enrich her life with these teachable moments.

When we went to Greece over the summer, I encouraged her to branch out and try new foods that she may have been hesitant to sample at home. Surprisingly, she liked several Greek pastries, such as tiropita and spanakopita. This led to a conversation about how people from other countries eat different foods as a part of their culture. Rather than being "weird," this is what makes each culture unique. Raising Emily as a globally minded person is important to me because I teach international students, and I would like her to have a greater appreciation for different cultures and languages. As a result, I approached our trip to Greece as an opportunity to expose her to the beauty of another country's customs, much as I do in the classroom when I facilitate a discussion among my students about customs in other cultures.

Try It!
Think about your own career and which skills you can apply to your relationship with your stepchild. Choose one skill you perfected in your career and apply it to one of your interactions with your stepchild.

Reflection
♥ What are some of your skills from either your career or your life that you could utilize in your relationship with your stepchild? What kind of skills or personality characteristics do people often compliment you on?

_____
_____
_____
_____

♥ Think back to a situation with your stepchild that you handled particularly well. What actions, on your part, contributed to the successful nature of the interaction? How can you transfer that to other situations?

_____
_____
_____

REMINDERS for next time

Day 20: Be yourself and show your stepchild your awesomeness.

Be yourself; everyone else is already taken.

-Oscar Wilde

Being yourself sounds great, but can be hard to do because suddenly you're in a new role that you're still trying to figure out. And you're still trying to decipher *who* you are in that role, so it can be hard to be yourself. You might feel like you need to be stricter in front of your stepchild, so that they take you more seriously as a parental figure. Or you might feel hesitant to say certain things in front of your stepchild because you don't want them relayed to the other household. As hard as this may be, try to forget about those things, and be the person that you've always been. Instead of focusing on roles or titles, be the silly or carefree person that your husband fell in love with. Just because you have a new title, doesn't mean that you have to reinvent yourself.

Remember that you can be an excellent role model for your stepchild and you can set the tone for your relationship. Even if you have a strained relationship with your stepchild, keep focusing on the things that you love to do and your relationship with your family members. Even if you never have a close relationship with your stepchildren, at least they can respect the person that you are. Keep modeling the behavior that you would like to see in your stepchild, and one day they might surprise you.

Try It!
Are you being true to yourself? Take a moment and write down some adjectives to describe you. If you're not sure, ask your friends for some help and ask them how they would describe your personality.

About Me

_____
_____
_____
_____
_____
_____
_____

Reflection

♥ Take a look at the adjectives that you wrote down. The next time you feel yourself getting upset in a situation, ask yourself: am I acting like myself or like the person I *think* I should be in this role? Why am I acting differently than I normally do?
_____
_____
_____
_____
_____

♥ What can I do to act more like myself?
_____
_____
_____
_____
_____

Day 21: Tune Your Stepchild out at Times.

I was taught that the way of progress was neither swift nor easy.
-Marie Curie

You know how parents have an uncanny ability to tune their children out at times? Yes, that's exactly what you need to try with your stepchild sometimes! I know this can be hard to do because we want to be a good stepmom and be attuned to our stepchild's needs, but that can also work against us. I found myself being hypersensitive to everything my stepdaughter said. *Wait, did she just say that I am not the best at doing hair? After all of the time that I spent on her hair, how dare she?!* Sometimes I would mention it to my husband later on, and he would have no idea what I was talking about. I'm not advocating letting your stepchild spout off and be disrespectful, but just let some of those small comments go. When I made a resolution to let some of it roll off my back, and not take everything personally, our relationship improved. She felt more comfortable around me and I felt better because I wasn't upset all the time. I learned that I don't have to respond to every comment a child makes.

Try It!
Try letting some of the minor comments go. Don't respond to everything that the child says.

Reflection
♥ What kind of comments does your stepchild make that bother you? Are these comments that you can let slide, or do you need to address them with her?

_____
_____
_____

♥ How do you handle it when your stepchild makes comments that are rude or inappropriate?

_____
_____
_____

Day 22: Ask your husband.

A recipe has no soul. You, as the cook, must bring soul to the recipe.

-Julia Child

"You're having a tough time? I had no idea! You seem to be doing a great job—Emily loves you and you've been such a good influence on her." Surprise and disbelief have been my husband's response a few times when I mentioned I was going through a rough patch, which caused me to reflect on things from his perspective. Were things going well? What was difficult for him about parenting with me, a stepparent? I decided to ask him and find out what advice he would have for me and other stepmothers in general. He mentioned that he would like me to feel more comfortable in acting like a parent. By acting more like a parent, he meant that he would like me to be more active in disciplining and punishing Emily. I explained that I would like to reinforce rules that are set, but I would like him to be the main disciplinarian as the biological parent. My husband also complimented me on passing on my good values and ethics to Emily.

When I asked another father, Dan, about the difference between parenting with a biological mother and a stepmother, he mentioned how biological parents often take each other for granted, expecting the other one to automatically take part in rearing the children. Whereas in parenting with a stepparent, the biological parent doesn't want to overwhelm the stepparent with childrearing duties. As the father of three children who is now parenting with a childless stepmother, Dan explained, "I feel pressure to try to keep everyone happy. Pressure to keep Sara (the stepmom) happy and pressure to keep the kids happy. Sometimes I feel like it's up to me to keep everything balanced." Dan's perspective gives us valuable insight into the difficulties that our husbands might be having in this situation.

Try It!
Ask your husband to give you some advice about how you're doing or how to handle his children. Remember that this might be hard for him to do, but just ask and try to consider his advice objectively. Alternatively, you can read some blogs or articles written by men who are remarried and co-parenting with their new wives. What advice do they give?

Reflection

♥ What kind of advice did your husband give you? Or what kind of advice did you find in articles or blogs? What do you think about that advice?

_____
_____
_____
_____
_____

♥ Can you incorporate it into your life or into what you're currently doing? Or should you write it down and consider it in the future when you're in a better frame of mind?

_____
_____

♥ What kind of difficulties has your husband been having with parenting? Has he been feeling pressure to keep everyone happy?

_____
_____
_____
_____

```
GOALS ...
1.
2.
3.
```

Day 23: Don't be afraid to ask for help.

Walk towards the sunshine, and the shadows will fall behind you.

-Mary Engelbreit

"This is a lonely, isolating job—being a stepmom—and it feels like no one gets it. Everyone gets moms. No one gets that stepmoms are second; second in everything, yet they love, support, care for, put drops in eyes, comfort crying children, curl and braid hair and remind children to do chores," Suzy, a stepmother of four children, explained. Just like Suzy, I remember when I first became a stepmother, I had similar feelings of being alone, like no one would understand what I was going through. I also had a hard time admitting to myself and others that I was struggling. I felt like they would see me as a failure, as a bad stepmother. However, the exact opposite happened as soon as I opened up to others. I felt an outpouring of love and support from other stepmoms, and it was in part through this circle of support that I was able to make it through those tough times.

One night, as I was leaving my yoga class, I was chatting with another woman in the class, April, and I happened to mention my stepdaughter. She was surprised to hear that I had a stepdaughter and told me that she had raised two stepdaughters. She gave me her phone number and told me to call her to set up a coffee date so we could chat. After an exceptionally hard day, I contacted her and we arranged to meet the following Saturday at a nearby coffee shop. We ended up talking for almost three hours! She came prepared with some advice and ideas that she had written down for me. I felt like a weight had been lifted as we talked because I was able to talk to her without judgment on her part for the way I was feeling or what I was experiencing. April was just one person who has helped me on my journey, but I will be eternally grateful for the time that she spent talking to me and encouraging me.

Another rock in my journey was a work colleague, Jennifer, who I was able to confide in about stepmothering issues when I found out that she was also a childless stepmother of one. When I was stressed out one Monday after a weekend with Emily, Jennifer encouraged me to find an activity that I would look forward to doing on the weekends. She confessed that she volunteered at the local aquarium every Saturday when her stepdaughter was growing up because she wanted some time to herself and, as an avid scuba diver, she loved being around all the fish. She also said that her husband and stepdaughter enjoyed that special time together on Saturdays, while she relished having the day to herself.

Try It!
Once you open up, you'll be surprised by the people that you find in the same position as you. I'm not suggesting that you pour your heart out to a colleague who is busy working on a report, or who has no desire to have personal conversations at work. Most parents like to talk about their children, so if you mention your stepchildren, you might find a kindred spirit in a class that you're taking, at work, or in the community. Try to find 2-3 people that you feel comfortable talking to and exchanging information about stepparenting. Also, look for a stepparenting class or group in your area and keep that information handy. If you're really struggling, sign up for it now, but if you don't feel like it's necessary right now, keep it handy for another time.

Reflection
♥ When you're having a bad day, what makes you feel better?
___
___
___
___

♥ Have you identified some "rocks" on your journey? Who can you talk to? Do you have different friends to talk to about different issues?
___
___
___
___
___
___
___
___

Day 24: Don't worry about what others think.

You wouldn't worry so much about what others think of you if you realized how seldom they do.

-Eleanor Roosevelt

One thing that you'll learn as a stepmom is that everyone will have an opinion about how you should do things, but the most important thing is what works for you and your family, so don't worry about what others think. You'll have to figure out some basic things, like what your stepchild should call you and your family. One stepmother, Jennifer, revealed that she likes being called "Bonus Mom" because "it makes me feel like I add to number of parents who care so much for this child." I was comfortable with Emily calling me by my first name, but I didn't know what she should call my parents. Should she call them Grandma and Grandpa? Or should she call them by their first names? In the end, I decided to talk to my parents and ask them what they felt comfortable with, since this was all new to them, too. I also talked to Emily separately about it. My parents wanted to treat her exactly as they do the other grandchildren, so they refer to her as their grandchild, while Emily chose to call them by their first names. Judy, a step grandparent to two children, likes to refer to them as her "bonus" grandchildren.

While this is just one example of an issue that will come up, others will surface, and when they do, instead of worrying about everyone else's opinion on the topic, find out what works for you and your family. This is especially important for us as childless mothers because oftentimes people feel like they need to share their parenting opinions with us because we don't have children of our own. Instead of focusing on what they think, first concentrate on what is best for your family.

Try It!
The next time that you go somewhere and find yourself worrying about what someone else thinks, stop yourself. Instead, ask yourself: is this relevant to the happiness and well-being of my family?

TRY IT!

Reflection
♥ Do you worry about what others think? If so, when do you find yourself worrying about what they think?
_____
_____
_____
_____
_____

♥ When do you feel that others are judgmental of what you're doing or the way that you're acting? How can you get past that feeling and/or ignore it? What is the best way to handle the situation?
_____
_____
_____
_____

Day 25: Give yourself time to love the children.

Be somebody who makes everybody feel like a somebody.

-Robby Novak, Kid President

One thing that I felt terrible about and didn't feel comfortable confessing to anyone was that I wasn't sure that I loved my stepchild. When I was part of a special writing group one summer, I even ended up writing about this because I felt so guilty that I couldn't actually tell anyone about it. The prompt was "I need to write about…" I'm sharing it with you because you might be able to relate to what I wrote.

I need to write about…
How hard it is to be a stepmother
To try to love a child
As my own
Without those inherent maternal feelings
Without the unwavering love a mother
Feels upon her child's birth
Trying, Trying, Trying
Guilty feelings
Always trying to compensate
To love in other ways
To appreciate little moments
Wide smiles, hugs given freely
A laugh, a playful pinch
Small moments that mean so much
I need to write about these things
Because they help me to heal.

Just writing these words down helped me breathe a sigh of relief. I even ended up sharing what I wrote in a small group because I figured that I was safe in sharing with my writing group. My fear was that a mother would judge me and think I'm a terrible person, incapable of loving a child. I certainly couldn't tell my husband how I felt. What would he think? If you're feeling the same way, realize that you're not alone and you shouldn't feel guilty about how you feel (or don't feel.) Just as loving a mate takes time, so does loving a stepchild. Don't feel like you have to instantly love your stepchild.

Start by finding some traits that you admire in your stepchild and try to focus on the positive attributes. Give yourself and your stepchild time and space to let love grow between you. If it doesn't grow, don't force it, and just try to appreciate those positive qualities that your stepchild possesses. One stepmother, Jennifer, summed it up with these words, "do not feel like you have to *love* your new child but do appreciate them for the interesting little individual that they are."

Conversely, loving your stepchild might come naturally to you, as it did for Liz, a stepmother of eleven years, as she explains, "I was never able to have my own children, so I was happy to be a step parent to fill that void. As I still tell Anthony on a regular basis, I did not give birth to you, but I love you like I did." Liz adds, "Anthony has made Mother's Day a very special day for me since he came into my life. He always gives me a beautiful card and writes the most amazing words that make me cry every year. Anthony and I have a very strong and loving relationship. He can always count on me to be there for him and support him."

Try It!
Take the same writing prompt "I need to write about…", give yourself 10 minutes, and write whatever comes to mind.

Reflection
♥ How do you feel about your stepchild? How do you express how you feel about your stepchild?
___
___
___
___

♥ What are some traits that you admire in your stepchild?
___
___
___
___

I need to write about...

Day 26: It's completely normal to feel kind of crazy at times.

A question that sometimes drives me hazy: am I or are the others crazy?
-Albert Einstein

Technically, this is for Day 26, but this can also be for any day that you might be feeling like you're from another planet. Taking on a child can be a stressful situation for anyone, so don't feel like you have to keep it completely together all the time. Don't lose hope if you have days when you feel like you're emotional, depressed, or just not yourself. Millions of women out there are in similar situations and are feeling the exact same way as you. How you overcome this feeling and let your true self shine is paramount.

Try to realize that this is a temporary feeling and will constantly be in flux. There will be good days, bad days, and maybe even some terrible days. The important thing is how you react to these days and handle the situations that come up. We won't always handle each situation with dignity and grace, as we might imagine when we're envisioning these situations, but that's life! I've had days where I wanted to stay in bed, engrossed in a good book, watch some mindless shows, or drink coffee and write. I just didn't feel like getting involved with the latest disciplinary issue with Emily.

If you feel like that from time to time, don't fret. Check out, refresh, and think about how you can tackle the situation with a better mindset in the future. Come back as a stronger person with greater resilience for next time.

Try It!
The next time that you're feeling really emotional, take a moment to realize that you're having a bad day and do something that makes you feel good. Read a chapter in that book that you love, or whip up a new dish that you've been dying to try out.

Try It!

_____
_____
_____
_____

Reflection

♥ What made you feel so emotional? Was there a trigger or were you just having a bad day?
_____
_____
_____
_____
_____
_____
_____

♥ What did you do to snap out of it? Were you able to snap out of it pretty quickly, or did it take a couple of days?
_____
_____
_____
_____
_____
_____
_____

Day 27: Think of all of the awkward situations as snapshots in the grand scheme of things.

You have to accept whatever comes, and the only important thing is that you meet it with the best you have to give.

-Eleanor Roosevelt

As a stepparent, you're going to face countless awkward situations, so you might as well get used to it and embrace these situations if you can. Picture the dance recital that your stepdaughter has been anticipating for weeks that you need to attend, along with your husband's ex-wife and her boyfriend. Of course, you might not all sit together, but you will need to make small talk during the intermission when you all want to snap a picture of the child. Small talk, as you know, can be really hard. What's a safe topic? *If I mention how pretty Emily looks, will Emily's mom take it the wrong way, since I was the one who did her make-up? I didn't intend for it to be a barb, but every statement can become emotionally-charged in these situations.* Also, think about the awkwardness from your stepchild's point of view. She wants everyone to be happy at her recital, so she'll wave at both sets of parents an equal number of times, so that neither one of them feels left out. And that's precisely why it's important in these situations to think about the happiness of your stepchild. Yes, it's uncomfortable for all of the adults involved, but this is really about the special moment in your stepchild's life.

Try to forget about the five minutes of stilted conversation, and focus instead on the happiness of your stepchild and this significant moment in their life. This moment is not about you; on the contrary, it's all about them. The time will fly by so fast, and you want them to have happy moments from their childhood where all of the adults were cordial to one another and came together for that important moment in their life. Everything else is inconsequential.

Try It!
The next time that you encounter an awkward situation, instead of focusing on how you feel, think about how your stepchild feels.

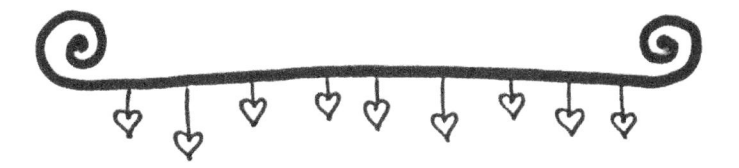

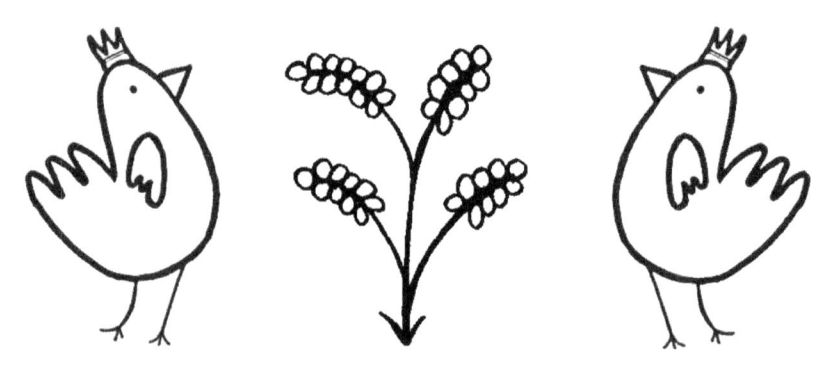

Reflection
♥ What awkward situations have you encountered? What made them so awkward? How did you react to the situations? How would you react differently in the future?
_____
_____
_____
_____
_____

♥ How do you think your stepchild and your husband felt?
_____
_____
_____
_____
_____

♥ What was a happy moment for your stepchild in this uncomfortable situation?
_____
_____
_____
_____

Day 28: Try to rise above it all.

You can often change your circumstances by changing your attitude.
-Eleanor Roosevelt

Ask yourself: will this matter in five years? If the answer is no, then don't waste your time and energy getting worked up about it. You have better things to do than sit around and worry about the latest annoyance from your husband's ex-wife. Arguments about trivial things such as which articles of clothing are going back and forth between households will happen all the time. For me, I found myself becoming involved in silly things, like getting upset when Emily argued about wearing a pair of shoes back to her mom's house or when she didn't want to decorate a Valentine's Day mailbox with me.

Try to keep things in perspective and stay your positive self. Don't become bitter and jaded, always talking about what your husband's ex-wife did now or the latest escapade involving your stepchild. We've all encountered those people and it's really easy to fall into that behavior. (I'm guilty of it, too!) You, on the other hand, have much better things to do with your time! Remember that I am referring to petty things that don't amount to much in the grand scheme of things. If it is a serious issue related to the health or well-being of the child, then the issue needs to be addressed with your husband and his ex-wife.

Try It!
When you feel upset about a situation involving your stepchildren and/or their mother, once again, ask yourself: will this matter in 5 years? If the answer is no, write it down or share it with a trusted friend, but don't dwell on it.

Reflection
♥ Can you think of a time when you were embroiled in an argument about petty things related to your stepchild? Why did the situation become so heated?

_____
_____
_____
_____

♥ How did you overcome this situation?
_____
_____
_____
_____
_____
_____

♥ How can you be the bigger person in these situations?
_____
_____
_____
_____
_____

REMINDERS for next time

Day 29: Step back.

Sometimes you don't realize you're actually drowning when you're trying to be everyone else's anchor.

—Author Unknown

Sometimes, you keep trying and trying without much luck and start to feel resentment towards your stepchildren and your husband. Step back and don't worry so much about them. Do what you need to do in order to keep your sanity. This is tricky because there is a fine line to walk between complete detachment and a safe distancing of yourself in order to handle the situation. Instead of getting upset over these situations, I decided to take a conscious step back in order to protect myself. I focused on other things that could use more of my attention, such as my passion for writing and photography.

By distancing myself, I could gather my strength and resilience for the next challenge that might present itself. The ironic thing is that I noticed that Emily was more drawn to me when I distanced myself, just as she is drawn to our "cool" cat, Garfunkel. She completely ignores our loving, ever-present dog, while seeking the affection of our often-hidden cat who couldn't care less whether he gets attention. I also found this to be true of her relationship with me when I took a clue from Garfunkel and distanced myself from her.

Try It!
The next time that you find yourself trying too hard and going nowhere, step back. Distance yourself and focus your energy on other things.

Reflection
♥ What happened when you stepped back? How did your husband and stepchild react when you stepped back?

_____
_____
_____
_____
_____

Day 30: What's next?

The true voyage of self-discovery lies not in seeking new landscapes but in having new eyes.
-Marcel Proust

Keep writing, reflecting, and experimenting. Take note of what works, what makes the situation better, and what makes you feel better. You'll be surprised. While you might be feeling disheartened now, in a few months, everything could be much better. Conversely, while you might be feeling pretty good right now, in a few months, that could all take a turn for the worse. I've found that being a stepmother can be much like riding a roller coaster, with constant highs and lows. The good news is that you'll never be bored!

No matter what happens, channel your positivity on those rough days, keep your support group close, and continue writing. I've found that on those difficult days, just writing down what happened and how it made me feel helps me to process what happened and serves as a frame of reference down the road. If I'm able to write it down and flesh out exactly why it hurt or upset me, I feel more at ease. On the great days, make sure you write down what made them great and also write down any "small victories" that happen. These "small victories" can be anything that you made someone in your family feel good, something to cherish later on. My most recent "small victory" happened when I took my stepdaughter to my friend's house to make homemade doughnuts and go swimming. When we got back home, she promptly sat down at the kitchen table and started quietly writing on a notecard. Pretty soon, she presented me with the note, which told me what a good time she had, thanking me for taking her and telling me that she loved me. This "small victory" warmed my heart. I'll draw on it on those rough days down the road.

Above all, remember why you started on this beautiful but challenging journey and think about how much stronger you are because of it. Raising a stepchild takes a special person with lots of love and patience.

Try It!
Buy a journal and start filling it with your thoughts, hopes, and dreams.

Reflection

♥ How have you evolved throughout this process? How are you going to keep moving forward on your journey?

_____
_____
_____
_____
_____

♥ What are some "small victories" that you are especially proud of?

_____
_____
_____
_____
_____

♥ What's next for you on your journey? What are you looking forward to?

_____
_____
_____
_____

Made in the USA
Las Vegas, NV
28 April 2023